PRAISING HIM
Through Your Pain

EVEN IN YOUR DARKEST NIGHT,
GOD IS STILL THERE

BARBARA L. DANIELL

WESTBOW
PRESS®
A DIVISION OF THOMAS NELSON
& ZONDERVAN

This book is a work of non-fiction. Unless otherwise noted, the author
and the publisher make no explicit guarantees as to the accuracy of
the information contained in this book and in some cases, names of
people and places have been altered to protect their privacy.

WestBow Press books may be ordered through booksellers or by contacting:

WestBow Press
A Division of Thomas Nelson & Zondervan
1663 Liberty Drive
Bloomington, IN 47403
www.westbowpress.com
844-714-3454

Because of the dynamic nature of the Internet, any web addresses or
links contained in this book may have changed since publication and
may no longer be valid. The views expressed in this work are solely those
of the author and do not necessarily reflect the views of the publisher,
and the publisher hereby disclaims any responsibility for them.

Any people depicted in stock imagery provided by Getty Images are
models, and such images are being used for illustrative purposes only.
Certain stock imagery © Getty Images.

All Scripture quotations are taken from the New King James Version®.
Copyright © 1982 by Thomas Nelson. Used by permission. All rights reserved.

All poems contained in this book, are authored by Barbara L. Daniell

ISBN: 978-1-6642-4470-2 (sc)
ISBN: 978-1-6642-4476-4 (e)

Print information available on the last page.

WestBow Press rev. date: 11/16/2021

CONTENTS

FOREWORD

This book is for anyone who loves and appreciates poetry; but more than that, for anyone who has experienced the sting, hurts, betrayals, difficulties, the confusions of life, and just life itself.

Inside this book lies the Answer and the Key of how to get over the wounds of life and how to "Heal" from them.

And not only that, but to know how it is possible and to know the reality of being made Strong in our weakness; receiving Acceptance, instead of allowing rejection to do its destructive work; having Light in our darkness; to know Singing, Dancing and Rejoicing, after we have known sadness and despair.

May you be richly, Blessed as, you read through the pages of this book; I know that the contents on the following pages, is something that everyone in the world can relate to, at some time or another. This little book is timeless and what was True years ago, is still True and Works, today – and what is True and Works today, will still be True and Work (to Heal our broken hearts) a thousand years, from now, to Give us a Victorious mind-set, in order to get over every negative attitude and emotional bondage that, the devil has tried to bring your way.

As you find your place in these pages, and your areas of relating to - **may the God of Abraham, Isaac and Jacob, Reveal His Personal Love, Power, Comfort and Peace to your mind, spirit and soul.**

And may you too, experience and *learn* to "Praise Him" through your pain; as you put your Trust in God, the sun will eventually, come out, your sorrow will be Turned to Joy and He Will Give you Beauty for your ashes!!

Be BLESSED!

ACKNOWLEDGMENTS

First, and foremost, I thank the Lord for His Awesome and truly, Unfailing Love and Mercy (and never giving-up on me).

I thank both my children Amy and Woodrow for always being there for "mom" - and having wonderful hearts. Like the rest of us - their "Faith" is still a work in progress (just like mine), and before things are all said and done - I know they will both Come Forth as Gold;

Along with my 2 precious granddaughters, who are amazing and continually have God's Grace & Favor upon their lives.

The LORD is Teaching all my children and their "PEACE" shall be great, as they Build their houses (lives) on the Rock (Jesus), instead of sinking sand; and they shall be mighty in the land.

To Kay Author who was my spiritual mother; and to my mother church Central Baptist Church of Hixson, TN with Dr. Ron Phillips (which is now known as Abba's House, with Pastor Ronnie Phillips, residing) - where all good things started on this journey of Victory.

This is where I first started learning about spiritual warfare, a little over 20 years ago.

Knowing about the Spiritual warfare that, comes against us, is absolutely crucial to having the Victory in this Christian walk.

We cannot be delivered from any demonic attack when we don't even understand that, it even exists. The Spirit of God began showing me who I am in Christ Jesus - for "who the Son has set free is Free indeed;" and it was here where the Lord introduced me to this act and experience of "Worship" on one Sunday night back in January of 2002, the first night of one of their awesome revivals, with Kelly Varner.

God truly came down and "Kissed" me that night, and for the first time, I truly "felt" God's Awesome Presence (although I did not realize it was His presence at that time) I just knew I was feeling His Great Love for me, and I as I stood there with hands raised toward Heaven, Singing Praises to Him, with tears of Affirmation, Comfort and Love literally streaming down my face, along with a hundred and something other people Worshipping God, also. It was Comforting, Reassuring, Strengthening and Purifying - and at that moment, He was more Real than I ever thought possible, and has Continued to be ever since (as I continue to Seek Him, Praise Him and Worship Him)! I have discovered He is waiting on us to "SEEK" His Face, and Call upon Him and it is then He will Answer us and Show us Great and Mighty things we do not know and that, He is a Rewarder of them that diligently Seek Him!

I AM ACCEPTED

GOD ACCEPTS ME

"FOR YOU ARE ACCEPTED
IN THE BELOVED"

EPHESIANS 1:6

GOOD PLANS

FOR I KNOW THE PLANS I HAVE FOR
YOU, SAYS THE LORD, PLANS TO
PROSPER YOU, AND NOT TO HARM
YOU, TO GIVE YOU A FUTURE AND A HOPE
JEREMIAH 29:11

HE SENDS ANGELS TO PREPARE ME

Exodus 23:20, 21

"Behold, I send an Angel before you to keep you in the way and to bring you into the place which I have prepared.

Beware of Him and obey His Voice; do not provoke Him, for He will not pardon your transgressions; for My Name is in Him.

22-But indeed if you obey His Voice and do all that I speak, then I will be an enemy to your enemies and an adversary to your adversaries. For My Angel will go before you and bring you in to the Amorites and the Hittites and the Perizzites and the Canaanites and the Hivites and the Jebusites: and I will cut them off,

24-You shall not bow down to their gods, not serve them, nor do according to their works; but you shall utterly overthrow them and completely break down their sacred pillars.

25-"So you shall serve the Lord your God, and He will bless your bread and your water, and I will take sickness away from the midst of you,

26-No one shall suffer miscarriage or be barren in your land; I will fulfill the number of your days.

27-"I will send My fear before you, I will cause confusion among all the people to whom you come, and will make all your enemies turn their backs to you.

28-And I will send hornets before you, which shall drive out the Hivite, the Canaanite, and the Hittite from before you.

29-I will not drive them out from before you in one year, lest the land become desolate and the beasts of the field become too numerous for you.

30-Little by little I will drive them out from before you, until you have increased, and you inherit the land.

31-And I will set your bounds from the Red Sea to the sea, Philistia, and from the desert to the River. For I will deliver the inhabitants of the land into your hand, and you shall drive them out before you.

32-You shall make no covenant with them, nor with their gods,

33-They shall not dwell in your land, lest they make you sin against Me. For if you serve their gods, it will surely be a snare to you."

GOD CAUSES ME TO REJOICE

HE CAUSES ME TO REJOICE-
BECAUSE HE SAID TO ME – LIVE

But let all those REJOICE who put their trust in You;
Let them ever shout for joy, because You defend them;
Let those also who love Your Name,
Be joyful in YOU. Psalm 5:11

(The first time I read this, after God led me to it - I read it literally for 9 days straight, crying every time just at the reality and awesomeness of it)

Ezekiel 16:1-9
Again the word of the Lord came to me, saying, "Son of man, cause Jerusalem to know her abominations, and say, 'Thus says the Lord God to Jerusalem: "Your birth and your nativity are from the land of Canaan; your father was an Amorite and your mother a Hittite. As for your nativity, on the day you were born, your navel cord was not cut, nor were you washed in water to cleanse you; you were not rubbed with salt nor wrapped in swaddling cloths. No eye pitied you, to do any of these things for you, to have compassion on you; but you were thrown out into the open field, when you yourself were loathed on the day you were born. And when I passed by you and saw you struggling in your own blood, I said to you in your blood, 'LIVE!' Yes, I said to you in your blood, 'LIVE!' I made you thrive like a plant in the field; and you grew, matured, and became very beautiful, your breasts were formed, your hair grew, but you were naked and bare. When I passed by

4

you again and looked upon you, indeed your time was the time of love; so I spread My wing over you and covered your nakedness. Yes, I swore an oath to you and entered into a covenant with you, and you became Mine, says the Lord God.

V9 -Then I washed you in water; yes, I thoroughly washed off your blood, and I anointed you with oil.

AWESOME, AWESOME, AWESOME

PLEASE OBEY THE VOICE OF THE LORD

Jeremiah 38:20
".....Please obey the Voice of the Lord which I speak to you. So it shall be well with you, and your soul shall live.

Isaiah 60:1
"Arise shine, For your light has come!
And the glory of the Lord has risen upon you.
v.2
"For behold, the darkness shall cover the earth, And deep darkness the people;
But the Lord will arise over you,
And His glory will be seen upon you."

Isaiah 59:19
So shall they fear the Name of the Lord from the west,
And His glory from the rising of the sun;

When the enemy comes in like a flood,
The Spirit of the LORD will lift up a standard against him.

v.20 The Redeemer will come to Zion,
And to those who turn from transgression in Jacob, says the Lord...

GOD REJOICES OVER ME

Zephaniah 3:17
The Lord your God is in your midst,
The Mighty One, will save;
He will rejoice over you with gladness,
He will quiet you with His love,
He will rejoice over you with singing.

Zephaniah 3:19
I will appoint them for praise and fame
In every land where they were put to shame.

Zephaniah 3:14
SING O daughter of Zion! Shout O Israel!
Be glad and rejoice with all your heart,
O daughter of Jerusalem!

v.15 The Lord has taken away your judgments, He has cast out
your enemy,
The King of Israel, the Lord, is in your midst; you shall see
disaster no more.

v.19-.....I will deal with all who afflict you.....

REJOICE O DAUGHTER OF ZION

Zechariah 8:9
"Thus says the Lord of hosts;
'Let your hands be strong,
You who have been hearing in these days these words by the
mouth of the prophets........'"

v.12 - For the seed shall be prosperous................

O house of Judah and house of Israel,
So I will save, and you shall be a blessing. Do not fear, Let your
hands be strong.

Zechariah 9:9
REJOICE GREATLY, O DAUGHTER OF ZION!
SHOUT O DAUGHTER OF JERUSALEM!

BEHOLD YOUR KING IS COMING TO YOU

Zechariah 2:5
For I, says the Lord, 'will be a wall of fire all around her, and I
will be the glory in her midst.'"

Zechariah 2:10-12

SING and REJOICE O daughter of Zion! For behold, I AM coming and I will dwell in your midst," says the Lord.

v.11 - And I will dwell in your midst. Then you will know that the Lord of hosts has sent Me to you.

v.12 - And the Lord will take possession of Judah.

WORD SHALL NOT RETURN VOID

Isaiah 55:11
So shall My Word be that goes forth from My mouth; it shall not
return to Me void, but it shall accomplish what I please,
And it shall Prosper in the thing for which I sent it.

Isaiah 63:7
I will mention the Loving Kindnesses of the Lord
And the Praises of the Lord....

Isaiah 63:4
For the day of vengeance is in My Heart,
And the year of My redeemed has come (Says, the Lord).

Isaiah 63:9
In all their affliction He was afflicted,
And the Angel of His Presence Saved them;
In His Love and in His pity He Redeemed them;
And He Bore them and Carried them,
All the days of their lives.

HE WILL HELP ME MAKE IT THROUGH THE NIGHT

Through the pain and through the tears
It is hard for me to see,
That the Almighty God, Creator of heaven and earth
Is interested in me.

In my hurt I can only feel
My tremendous loss, oh how real;
But if I could only see from where I stand,
That He has a Will and a Plan,
For Something Bigger, Better and more Grand.

If by Faith I could Trust His Heart
To see that He has my best interest as part
Of the Bigger Picture I cannot see,
Trusting that He Cares for me.

Lord Help me to Trust You
No matter what;
You have never failed
Your children yet.

You are Faithful, You are True,
Even when the rains begin to fall
And I cannot see through -
I will Trust You through it all.

And when my heart feels weak,
And my days and future look bleak,
When the pain just will not stop,
And my life and world are being rocked
I WILL TRUST YOU!!!

He will do me no wrong
For His Choices are Right,
And His Loving Grace and Care
Will Take me through the night.

And when life just gets so hard,
And we cannot see ahead,
We must look through the eyes of Faith,
And Believe what God has Said.

He makes no mistakes,
He is Faithful and True-
He has a Future, a Hope and a Plan
Just for you.

So Hang on, and Press in
Till the morning has Come,
And the rough journey will end;
The rains will stop,
The winds cease to blow,
But give it ALL YOU HAVE GOT,
And the Victory you Will Have, to Show.

So, when you cannot see "His" Plan,
And you do not understand,
Know that God Involves "Himself"
In the affairs of man;
He is Working still-

Oh how Powerful, and oh how Real
To Reveal His Mighty, Awesome power, And His Omnipotent,
Ruling, Reigning and Strong Hand!

Isaiah 41:9-13

v.9 - "...You are My servant, I have chosen you and have not cast you away:

v.10 - "Fear not for I AM with you; be not dismayed, for I AM your God. I will Strengthen you, yes, I will Help you, I will Uphold you with My righteous Right Hand.

v.11 - "Behold, all those who were incensed against you shall be ashamed and *disgraced*; They shall be nothing, and those who strive with you shall perish."

v.12 - "You shall seek them and not find them - Those who contend with you. Those who war against you shall be as nothing.

v.13 -"For I, the Lord your God, will Hold your right hand, Saying to you, 'Fear not, I Will Help you.'"

Jeremiah 29:11

"'For I Know the Plans I have for you', Declares the Lord, 'Plans to Prosper you, and not to harm you; Plans to give you a Hope and a Future'."

HERE IT COMES AGAIN

Why this lonely hell
I find myself in?
Every time I see a light
Here it comes again.

Here comes the rain, again -
Why?
Am I meant for such a rain?
Here it comes again,
A pain
Of the soul and mind...

It feels so wrong,
But yet it seems so right -
A time to express Your awesome Might:
Something I was meant to do -
To tell of You.

Can You be seen in this night?
The dark and lonely night?
Is Your great and mighty Hand there,
To help me anywhere?
Yes, You said Your Righteous Right Hand
Would be there
To strengthen, uphold and to guide
To help in the slippery time
So that I would not slide
On these slopes
That take out a lot of folks.

It's true -
No matter where I go
Your Grace and Love
Is always there to show;
Though I make my bed in hell,
Though I go to the deepest sea
You seem to always be there with me....

Even though it keeps on coming
So does Your awesome grace
And Your love overshadowing anything alarming
And Your peace so amazing...

So, let the rains come -
As long as YOU are there with me -
I know now, that You Faithfully
Will Sustain,
And Take Good Care of me,
Because You Love me.

THE KIND THAT KEEPS

I want to feel Your Grace
I want to see Your Face
I want to feel You Mercy
I want to know Your Love
The Kind that Holds you
When you fall.

I feel Your Grace
I see Your Face
And I feel Your Mercy
I know Your Love
The kind that Holds me when I fall
The kind that Holds me when I fall – still.

The kind that keeps me from falling
When I Call on You Name
For Your Mercy, and Your Grace - still.

The Kind that Keeps me from falling
When I Call on Your Name
For Your Mercy, And for Your Grace - still.

MENTOR ME - COVER ME

Bring me a mentor Lord
To speak into my life - I will listen and believe.

What do You want from me
I'm trying, but I still need Your Help,
Can I go any further on this trail
By myself?
It's not exactly as though I'm frail,
For I have learned to Lean on You
This You have taught me to do -
But I need Wisdom from another
That has already been down that road,
Please Lord, Help me Carry this load.

Bring me out -
I've been alone too long;
You know, Oh You know how alone...
You know how You are my SONG
You are my Rock
To You I belong,
You Give me a Song,
A New Song -
A song of Deliverance,
A song of Freedom,
A song of Mercy,
That You have Shown me,
From a life that has been full of failures,
And misery;

Yet, You have Chosen me -
Even before I was formed in my mother's womb
You knew me and chose me
For some reason,
To show Your Mercy and Your Glory and Your Love -
When the Evil One for so long,
Told me I was not loved, That I was nothing,
But he was wrong -
In my mother's womb he tried to claim me;
But You Caimed me before he did -
To God be the Glory!!!

HIS MESSENGERS

He sent one of His blessed messengers,
To me today -
To tell me that I am on my way;

That it's not hopeless or useless,
As many have said,
But that I will reap if I faint not,
His Spirit said.

THE LORD STOOD BY ME

"Everyone deserted me, but the Lord stood by me."
2 Timothy 4:17

HOLD ON

I Hear You say to me,
"Everything's going to be alright -
Hold on, Hold on,
Just Wait and See,
Hold on tight,
Just Keep Holding on to Me."

A REVELATION

A Revelation is a Truth of God,
Delivered by the Spirit of God,
To your heart
That will Change your soul
And life forever!

KILL YOUR AGAGS

I do not want to be,
Like disobedient Saul,
Who made many enemies to run -
But then on his own sword,
He did fall,
Because in truth he did not answer Your call.
He was told to kill his Agag,
His enemy - told by Your Command,
He chose not to follow through on the plan,
And the bleating of the sheep
Were heard, And Your anger and wrath were stirred -
But yet, Saul later said
"Oh Lord, have I not obeyed Your Word?" (1 Samuel 15:13)
Only to the half,
And not to the full,
Disobedience incurred God's wrath,
He was a fool,
And disobeyed God's Voice,
He made a very poor choice,
And for that,
He died.

What are your Agags? What are mine?
Sometimes, we need to walk the line,
We better make sure
That we follow His Plan,
Or we could end up
Like Lot's wife,
Who turned into a pillar of salt,
To stand.

IT WILL COME BACK TO YOU

I will come back and bless you,
For it is GOD that is Faithful and True,
For all that we say and do -
I will not forget you!!

Like the lepers of ten,
Only one, leaving nine
Returned to say, "thank You",
For being so kind,
For giving me your time,
For helping me
Be on my way,
For helping me to discover a better and brighter day;
For helping me to find a better way -
For pointing me in the right direction,
Helping me to find consolation -

Thank you for letting God use you so faithfully,
Thank you for giving of your time so freely;

It just reminds me that all that we do,
Will always, always be Rewarded,
If we will only stay true -
For the Lord is faithful and not slack
Concerning His Promises,
For everything we do,
Be it great or small,
Will all come back
To me and to you,
To us all.

THANK YOU

Thank You that You call me friend,
That You have Said to me, It will be alright in the end,
Thank You that You Guide me with Your eye
Thank You that You did not let me die:

For You have a Purpose and a Plan for my life-
Thank You that You have it all Worked out;
I've said before, I'm ready to fly,
You said, "you will live and not die
To tell all that I Have Done".

You're so Awesome, Lord
You've Convinced me of this
And my soul knows right well,
You are the Best.

I hardly have words enough to express
How great You have been to me,
Through the years I have seen
That You have always been with me,
That You have given the Angel of the Lord,
To Save and Deliver me,
And Has Been with me
All the days of my life.

The devil he could not kill me,
And he is trying, still -
But he is a liar
I am not a buyer
He will not succeed in Jesus Name;

For I am God's domain
And I will Obey Him,
And eat the fruit of the Land.

For I Believe that I have been Called,
For such a time as this,
To help Set the Captives free,
To Help them See
That You Want to Open the prison doors,
Of their lives and more.

You have Brought me
From ashes to Beauty,
And others, this they see -
And truly give God the Glory,
For You Can and Will Do the Same for them,
If only they will Believe.

HE GUIDES MY STEPS

You truly Guide my steps
Along the way,
Just like You Said,
You would everyday -

There is no mistake in what I feel,
It's based on Your Spirit,
Your Word and Your Power,
And it's so real -
You are raising up many,
For such an hour;

You Govern in the affairs of man,
And this Includes me,
I know many, many powerful prayers,
Have been prayed for me,
For Your Spirit and power to rest upon me,
From the hearts of Your anointed -

And it would not surprise me,
That they have asked the Lord of the harvest,
To send me forth,
As well,
Into the field,
For You have a purpose
And a Plan for them,
If only they Believe,
So they can KNOW,

That Your Blood for them was spilled,
So that to them,
You can Become so real!

I strive to do everyday,
The things I hear Your Spirit Say,
Knowing that You govern in the affairs of man,
Knowing that for me You have a plan;
Knowing that the Thoughts You Think toward me,
Are Good and not evil,
To Give me a Future,
And a Hope -
To Do me Good and not harm -
This has Brought Revival!

The things that I have Heard and Seen,
Were no accidents or mistakes,
You Guided my steps that way,
To Helped me Believe.

HELP ME TO MAKE IT

When am I going to feel relief
When am I going to be Loved?

Time is short
And my heart cries out -
Help me to make it, Lord
Help me to make it.

My mind cries out
Life is too much -
But my heart cries
Lord, You are Enough;

I hear Him saying
You WILL make it My child
Just Hold on a little while -
Hold on a little longer,
Even when all creation cries out
"They wrong her,"
Even when creation cries out
"They wrong her."

For so long -
The wrong keeps going on,
But just hold on, My child Hold on --

I See your pain, I See your tears
I See your wrong all these years -
But I AM Faithful, I AM True
I AM about to Come to you

My Reward is with Me
And My Salvation is Near.

Do not faint and do not quit
I AM your Reward
Just wait and see,
I AM Everything that you have ever Hoped to be.

MANIFESTED SOON

It's going to be Manifested soon,
It's going to all be Manifested soon,
All that You've Promised
All that You have Said;

All the prayers that I've prayed
All the nights that I have stayed,
Stayed up late Seeking Your Face
All the times I have cried out for Your Grace;

It's our Faith that matters to You
Even though I cannot see You,
I feel You, I know You Hear me,
And You Answer me.

You said to a woman once,
"Woman your Faith has made you whole".
And to another, "Whatever, you desire is done
Because your Faith is great";

You have Said to me
"Daughter of Zion you are Free,
Daughter of God Believe in Me,
Do not be afraid of the coming storm -
For I AM with you, I AM Jehovah Shama
I AM always there, I AM Bringing you along -
Remember when I Told you,

And the Message you just had to share -
You must be Strong,
Believe Me;
And you must keep your Song."

For out of Zion comes not only
A Beauty that none other can touch -

But out of Your Presence
Your Brush has Stroked,
A Perfection of Beauty and Wholeness,
For others to see,
That Your Grace and Holiness,
Has Bestowed on me.

For out of Zion
The Perfection of Beauty Comes,
God Will Shine Forth -
Oh daughter of the King REJOICE!
He is your King Worship before Him -
Worship Him, Worship Him, Worship Him!

MY SONG - MY REWARD

You have become my song,
And my Salvation,
When I cried unto You,
You began giving revelation;
You heard and answered my prayer,
And began making everything NEW!
And now, I know that YOU are everywhere!
You are truly in all that I say and do!

And because of this,
I will always worship and Praise You,
Because You said to my spirit,
And I do not want to miss it,
"I AM doing a NEW thing,
Can you not see it?"

Yes, I see it,
I feel it, I hear it,
I want to be a part of it -
For YOU have chosen me before my birth -
And all that other "stuff",
YOU have allowed to come my way,
Your Spirit and Your Power
And Your Love,
At it just puffs;

Even though, I know,
That through all our pain,
You feel our affliction,
You see the rain,

Your Heart is touched,
With our grief -
I now know that You LONG
To give us Relief -
You LONG to give us a SONG;

YOU are my SONG,
YOU are my Reward,
YOU are why I hold on,
For so long - With YOU I am never bored:
Yes, YOU are my Reward.

THE VIRTUOUS WOMAN

10) "Who can find a virtuous woman? For her price (Worth) is far above rubies.

11) The heart of her husband safely trusts in her; so he will have no lack of gain (or, no need of spoil)

12) She does him good and not evil all the days of her life.

13) She seeks wool and flax, And willingly works with her hands.

14) She is like the merchant ships, She brings her food from afar.

15) She also rises while it is yet night, And provides food for her household, And a portion for her maidservants.

16) She considers a field and buys it: From her profits she plants a vineyard.

17) She girds herself with strength, and strengthens her arms.

18) She perceives that her merchandise is good, and her lamp does not go out by night.

19) She stretches out her hands to the distaff, And her hand holds the spindle.

20) She extends her hand to the poor, Yes, she reaches out her hands to the needy.

21) She is not afraid of snow for her household, For all her household is clothed with scarlet.

22) She makes tapestry for herself; Her clothing is fine linen and purple.

v.25) Strength and honor are her clothing; She shall rejoice in time to come.

26) She opens her mouth with wisdom, And on her tongue is the law of kindness.

27) She watches over her household, And does not eat the bread of idleness.

28 (Her children rise up and call her blessed, Her husband also, And he praises her.

29) Many daughters have done well, But you excel them all.

30) Charm is deceitful and beauty is vain, But a woman who fears (trusts in) the Lord, she shall be praised.

31) Give her the fruit of her hands,

And let her own works praise her in the gates." Provers 31:10-22 and 25-30

MY PRECIOUS DAUGHTER

My precious daughter
Where do I begin
There's so much there
From without
From within;

Ever since you were born
I wrote a beloved poem to you
With your beautiful eyes so blue
I knew right then you were so special
I just had to try and pen
And relate as you would nestle.

I said then I didn't know where life would lead
Or how things would turn
Or how you would cleave;

As it has been,
I have made so many mistakes
That you have had to suffer from -
Lord, that's hard on a mother's heart,
How that takes her song.

You are such a powerful woman,
This you are not quite sure of,
But know this,
That others know,
And they are quite jealous of -

Remember, what you heard
The day we were finally able to attend
The woman's conference I kept begging you to go to -
And you went the last day, at the end?

Remember, the fireball lady that had so much to say,
She had a comical streak but didn't delay,
She spoke the truth,
I was so glad you could hear
About the battle raging,
She tried to make it clear -
It's not even about us,
But about the Treasure within,
This is where the struggle begins;
I'm not certain if you could Understand, yet,
What it's all about -
The fight without,
And the fight within?
It wars against your Treasure within!

The devil he is such a liar -
I know so many of his lies all too well,
He just wants to take you to hell -
But he can't have you, in Jesus Name,
For you are by God already Claimed;

Before you were Formed in your mother's womb
God, He Knew you,
And even Calls you by name -
Even before you Know Him,
And He Girds you and Strengthens you,
Even when you don't quite Understand;

But in the middle the Battle rages,
It even feels like it's the War of the ages;

My God, what a burden this is to carry,
I feel that I am the only one carrying this load,
This potential bode,
And moving things along -
It can really be scary;

Dear Lord, help me be Better
So that I can Help my daughter,
For I Know she is struggling
And probably feels so very alone -
I Persevere for such a long time
Doing well,
Then I seem to just let things go,
Tempted to think, "oh time will tell."

Help me Dear Lord,
For I can't keep this up,
Come Lord, Intervene
And Fill our empty cups;
And I Will Keep this up,
As long as I have to,
For You are my Strength and my Strong Tower,
Father God, give me Your Power.

What goes wrong
To make us lose our song?
Give me someone to come along,
And help me to carry this load,
For I am truly the strong one,
And on me everything is bestowed.... this weight and burden I feel,
Oh, this is so real,

Please cause others around me to Believe,
And add prayer partners and friends to me;

Send someone into this harvest field of hers
To Minister You Grace and Your Word,
This is what You said to pray for,
So You Know that is needed
And what Needs to be Heard.

Open her heart to Know
What must be Heeded.

Thank You ahead of time, Lord -
By Faith I Receive and Claim
Your Prophetic Word,
That You would Pour out Your Spirit
Upon my son and daughter
And that You would Teach them Your Word -

That the Words You have Put in my mouth
You would also Put in theirs -
And this Covenant YOU have Made with me,
They too would become Heirs;

And that the Words in our mouths
That YOU have Put there
Would not depart out of mouths
With our children and grandchildren
To Share,
From this time forth and
Forever more.

OPEN YOUR HEART

Open your heart,
Open your heart
By Faith,
By Faith open your heart,
Before it's too late,
And you will Live!!!!!

You will Live,
He, Jehovah Sabaoth says: LIVE, LIVE -
He Feels your pain,
Don't you understand, don't you understand
He Feels your hurt,
And He Wants to Hold your hand,
He Wants to Lift you Up off the sinking sand!!

He has Told you many times, in Love,
That He has an Awesome and Wonderful Good Plan;

But you must take a Stand,
You must not sit there till you die,
ARISE OH DAUGHTER -
No longer sigh!!
Arise oh daughter, You don't have to sigh -
Don't you Understand,
He Who sits in the Heavens
Hears when you sigh??
He Feels your pain,
And hurts when you hurt -
This He has told me once then twice, again;

He Knows where you are,
And is patiently Waiting
For you to Come to Him -
For He has already been Coming to you
And you have been "hiding" – And even running.

But the Time is NOW,
For you to say,
"Blessed is he or she who comes in the Name of the Lord,"
And He will quickly Come to you with His Favor, Grace and
Reward!
For He Wishes and Desires for you to Seek His Face,
And you will Find Him and a Treasure forever more!!

And I promise you,
You will no longer be bored,
Lost or dismayed,
Or ever again feel (permanently) displaced,
If you seek His Face,
Because He will Lead and Guide you continually
By His Grace!!

For the God of Abraham, Isaac and Jacob
Died for you and Rose again,
And is NOW Calling to you,
Saying I Want to be your King
Take Me by My Righteous Right Hand
And I will Cause you to Stand and Sing.

Open your heart, Open your heart to Me!
For it means Everything!

Do it, do it NOW!
Let your heart Bow
To ME, Says the Lord Jehovah Nissi,
And I will be your Covering
And you will See,
I Will Give you Life
Like no other
And I Will Give it Abundantly!!!

PROMISES FOR MY CHILDREN AND GRANDCHILDREN

For the LORD Shall Teach all my children
And Great shall be their PEACE!
In their struggles of life, they shall find ease
That did not come, naturally, but from Thee.

For they will soon Know
That God is with them
Everywhere they go,
Never to leave them, never to forsake them –
This Faith and Confidence they
They will Have in order to Show.

They Will Know that they are Chosen by You, Lord,
And when the evil-one spits: "who do you think you are?"
They will Use Your Word, their Sword –
It will be in them to reply, "I am Accepted by Jesus,"
That is why.
"I am His star, He Hears me when I sigh –
He Made me for a Good Purpose and Plan,
I am His Masterpiece
Created by His Hand.

He now, Fights all my battles, instead of me fighting them alone;
He Speaks to my heart,
And Gives me a Song.

I Can Do anything and everything He Tells me to Do,
As long as I Look to Jesus and Take His Que;

Old things are Passed away
And Behold, all things are Made NEW;
I am Strong and Courageous to Take the Land,
For He Guides me (now) with His Almighty, Omnipotent,
Righteous, Right Hand.

I am no longer the person I used to be,
The old man inside of me is gone, for sure,
My sins are in the deepest sea and I am Pure.
I am now Pressing Forward to New heights,
Focused on the Prize of the High Calling in Christ –
For the Blood of Jesus
Has Washed me Clean and Made me NEW!!
He Has a Good Plan for me that I Will Step into!

Now, I have a Future and a Real Hope,
No longer do I have an empty, disappointing hope,
But one of Comfort, Guidance & Promise
Given by God Himself;
He Holds me by His Righteous Right Hand
And now I can Stand –
Stand on the Promises, Stand for what is Right,
And now I can Fight –
I Stand with my Armor on,
For God is my Song!

So, get away from me, you father of lies,
You murderer from the beginning –
I resist you and now, you have to flee,
For I am now among those who BELIEVE:

Believing ON the Lord Jesus Christ,
I will Live and *NOT* die – This is Who I am
And this is Why!!"

ARISE O LEADER

He is doing it -
He is Pouring out His Spirit,
He is here
And He is pouring out His Spirit
On you and on me;

Thank You for considering me -
But why me?
What do You have for me,
What do You want me to do?

Arise O Leader
Arise O Head
And lead her -
For if the head be sick
The whole body is sick...

Let His Glory been seen in you
And be willing to say and do
Whatever HE Says to Do:
Arise O Leader.

For precious lives are at stake,
Do not stop half way!!
Do not settle
For mediocrity -
Keep Pushing, keep Pursuing
Keep Pressing
Into what His Spirit Tells you to Do -
Then you will not go wrong,

Then you will not cause harm -

And if not,
Then you will cause others to lose their Song,
And make their journey, ah, so long -
And end up causing great harm.

Remember, if you are not gathering to His Great Name,
Then you are scattering -
And you are the reason
For their confusion -
So quit passing the blame,
This truly is no game...
There is more to this than you and your ego
Will ever be able to tell -
As folks are dying everyday
And dropping into hell;
And Christians are being led astray
By your deceitful, proudful way;

But God is Watching,
And Listening to and Hearing every word,
Even when you think it does not matter
And that you have a handle on the greater;

He keeps in silence for awhile,
But do not mistake that for His Smile -
As He said that He will Rebuke you, now,
For your hypocritical
And lying ways;

And bring His Hand of judgment on you
For all your many days
Of leading His people astray -

He does not take it lightly -
So, take Heed O Leader
What you say,
For God is most certainly Listening,
And Watching
Every single day!

And remember,
He said that those who give Him Praise,
Bring Him Honor
All the days,
And Glorifies Him,
In all their ways...

So, be careful who you mess with
You so called religious person with no Righteous Fruit,
Be not of a double mind and heart,
Desiring man's approval;
God's Agenda is not ours,
His Thoughts are not our thoughts
Nor His Ways our ways -
The things we hold high
Are many times what He Passes by –

I Want to be Part of all those who
Glorifies Him in all they Say and Do!
Giving all of our Praises to God Above,
Who absolutely Dwells in the Praises of His People,
Who Walk in Genuine, Pure Love
Worshipping in His Temple

Is it any wonder
That the Enemy of mankind,
Fights tooth and nail

And brings the forces of hell,
To come against the Songs that we sing -
God Demands the Praise,
That He is so Worthy of
Be Brought to Him
All of our days....

Again, He Inhabits the Praises of His people -
Shout His praises in the Temple,
Sound the Battle-Cry,
For short is the hour
And many weary souls do sigh,
Saying, where is their King -
Oh, Shout, Rejoice oh people of God -
And SING, SING, SING!!!

For this is God's Battle
And He will Fight for you -
Or against you -
So Sound the Battle-Cry,
But you MUST do What He Says to Do,
And not what your fear dictates -
Go to His Spirit,
Do not hesitate;
For it's not by man's might or power
But by His Spirit, Says the Lord of hosts -
And His Spirit will Lift up a Standard against the evil-one,
When he comes in like a flood -
And the gates of hell will not prevail,
The gates of hell will not prevail!

For God Desires His Grace and Beauty
To you to Impart -
If you would only let Him -

To have an undivided heart,
Fully and wholly Devoted
To Him,
So that others could See Him
And not you -
So that He could Show Himself Strong
In these last days
Where there is so much wrong -
And weak and double ways.

Be Brave and be True
Arise O Leader,
And Do what God is Telling you to Do
Arise, Arise
O man of God
If that is truly what you want to be -
God is Looking for you,
He is Looking for me -
For such a time as this -
Do not let it pass you by,
Arise Oh Leader -
In Jesus Name!

MY SON, MY FRIEND

My son, my friend
I'm sorry you were offended,
And I'm the one who offended you,
But in all honesty
I know that I am right
About the the thing that you and I talked about last night -
I sometimes just don't know how to say it more gently...
You keep on insisting -
You should not be resisting...
I've been through this
And I understand where it leads,
What's dead and what's Alive
What Works and what's a lie;

You are such an amazing person to me,
And such an awesome son
Is so clear to see -
We have such great times together,
And when we do find time
In these incredibly busy days;
We have had such a bonding,
We seem to understand one another

Like no one else does.
We have had such moments of laughter,
You're really quite funny, you know -
You are so good with people
Everywhere you go
It shows -
You are so smart,

And I am not just speaking from a mother's heart,
Your intellect is so high
You could literally be anything,
You could soar and fly -
If you just keep on dreaming,
Don't let your Dreams die,
And they will Come to Pass by and by.

I just want you to know how very proud I am of you,
Keep Pressing, keep Pursuing
And above all keep God first!
For if you do like I did
And you leave Him out,
And do your own thing,
After awhile, You won't even be able to Sing -
Even though you think you're choosing Right
A person will mess up,
And find themselves in the dark and lonely night,
So frustrated you won't even know what to do.

So, just put Jesus first
And be so in Love with Him
And then you will find He is so in Love with you -
And see that He truly Fulfills from within,
And stay away from sin.
And you will not have the need to go after other gods
Be them little or be them big,
Do not dig wells that are empty and dry
And are worthless and have no value
And that eventually, cause us to sigh!

I know it's not all just cut and dry,
There is so much to this life.
And the devil hates us so much,

He comes to steal, kill and destroy,
And he is such a lie...

But you have to know his strategies
And that takes a bit,
But when you have a hunger for God
And want to spend time in His Word,
You will truly develop even more grit;
Then take precious and crucial time to talk to Him
Everyday of your life, a lot -
And be sure to thank Him for loading you down with His
Benefits,
And for all that you have got;
He will Lead you and Guide you
And you will be so amazed -

Remember to put yourself in an Anointed environment,
For we soon become what we put into us,
And Faith comes by hearing and hearing by the Word of God,
And He honors His Word more than His Name-
Imagine that;

And one last thing,
Learn to trust Him with all your heart,
And just like Mary the mother of Jesus said,
About Jesus himself:
"Whatever He says to you, Do"
This must be in your life and in your heart,
If you are to succeed and know what and when and how to do
Things that come at you...
Knowing that He Governs in the affairs of man -
And He said Himself this is His Plan,
That when His people Trust Him
He will quickly go after those who despise that man,

And no weapon formed against you will prosper,
And every tongue that rises against you in judgment
He will condemn -
Now that, my son, is a Plan!

MY SON

My son
You have the ball
Now run with it -
But not only run
But make sure you know Where you are headed
And Who you are listening to.

Make Certain you are not like the man on the field
Who finally obtained the ball,
And the fans from the stands
Were, standing as they would call.

Oh, they are so cheering me on
I can hardly take it,
Isn't life good
I'm going to make it.
No matter what I have to do,
Who says I can't do it my way
You just have to focus,
I can't listen to what you Say -

But little did he know
That he was going the wrong way!
And whether he drops the ball at this point
Or scores a touchdown,
Really doesn't matter -
Because you see,
He was running the wrong way!

So, don't be flattered by the wrong person,

Don't Listen to them or you will worsen.
But you (already) Have Spiritual Ears to Hear,
You are Listening to Wise & Godly advice –
And that's what Matters, especially, year after year!
God Can Trust you with Good Instruction,
And that will only Grow and Grow,
To Lead you in the Right Direction!

Remember that, God Takes each wrong turn we make,
And Turns it for our "Good,"
This is a Truth I've Learned through the years –
Even when I have not done what I should.
This is an Invaluable TRUTH that will Comfort & Guide you
And if you Let it, It Will FOREVER Abide with you!
It will Give you PEACE, instead of losing your mind –
It will Give you HOPE, instead of thinking, "Well, I blew it again,
There's no hope this time!"
HE'S WORKING ALL THINGS OUT FOR YOUR GOOD,
Because you are Called of Him and you Love HIM.
(This is an Eternal Truth – it is not a lie; it is True, Believe it!)

You will (Continue) to Get Stronger and Stronger each day,
As you Fill your mind and heart with what the Lord Has to Say;
For the Anointing Breaks every yoke,
And every bondage that tries to hold us down –
You might feel as if you're going to drown!
But Keep PRAYING and Looking UP –
I Promise you – God Will Fill your Cup!!
And your Dreams Will Come to Pass,
It's not too late –
Keep TRUSTING GOD and BELIEVING
And HE Will Bring it to Pass!

Commit your Dreams and Desires to HIM and HE Will be the One that Brings it to Pass –
(You Do your Part and He'll Do His – And More than you can imagine). Amen!

THE LORD WILL TEACH YOU

He will Instruct you and Teach you in the way you should go;
He will Guide you with His Eye.
Do not be like the horse or like the mule,
Which have no understanding,
Which must be harnessed with bit and bridle,
Else they will not come near you, but only pass you by.

Receive Understanding, Get Wisdom – And with all you have
got, get those two things – It means A LOT!
If you SEEK you Will FIND!
Then you will not be left behind!
God Will Honor you SEEKING HIM – It's your only Hope – it's
the only Hope for any of us!
And the Captivity He Leads us into, you can Become Strong right
in the midst of it –
I Give you Good Instruction – whatever you do, don't resist it!!
And in time, the Angel of the LORD Will See that you are
"Persevering."
And I Promise you that, it will mean your Victory – your Freedom.
And you Can begin living your long awaited Dreams –
Actually, your Calling – You just think they're deeply buried
desires,
When they're really your Destiny from someplace Higher!!
God Ordained Desires (Bridges, land, buildings) no telling what
He Has for you in your living!

My Prayer:

And Remember -

All your Children shall be Taught by the LORD,

And Great shall be the Peace of your Children.

The Anointing Breaks every yoke and bondage,

So, Go after HIS Anointing – Let the Most High and His Spirit Anoint your head with Oil

Then you Can Have a Second Chance to live life – to *really* Live life and be Free to Fulfill

your Dreams and Calling;

You only pass this way once –don't waste it.

Rely upon and TRUST IN THE LORD and He Will Lead you out – And then Lead you In!

(into those Dreams to be Fulfilled).

I Promise you – I do not tell you a lie;

I urge you to Keep Believing in the Lord, every single day and you will live and not stray – you will not die early, but Fulfill all your days! Amen.

THE BLOOD OF JESUS

The Blood of Jesus Covers me,
That Blood of Jesus Covers my family,
This is my plea -
It Covers me and my family;

I'm NOT afraid, I will NOT fear,
I know that Jesus - He is here,
Sabbaoth Is HIS Name -
Lord of Hosts,
He has not changed!

I'm in Covenant,
I'm not afraid of the darkness,
For I am in Covenant,
It Shows me the Light,
And everything is Right.

The Blood of Jesus Covers us,
The Blood of Jesus Protects us,
And the Angel of Lord
Will Chase that devil away,
The Angel of the Lord will Knock them down,
Turn them around and Make them run away!

Hallelujah, Hallelujah, Hallelujah!

JESUS DIED FOR THAT

Every smoke of crack, every drink of liquor, (in your pain or in your emptiness) every fowl cursing, vulgar word that came out of your mouth - Jesus died for that. Every bit of strife and evil that came from your heart and your actions; Every look of pornography; every indiscretion; every doubt of God's Goodness & Love, every rejection of His Mercy from above, every act of rebellion against God, every independent attitude against God's Will; every self-righteous & religious attitude and proud & stout heart...JESUS DIED FOR THAT!!!

But the Spirit of God will Break every yoke, Free you of every bondage and Loose every chain that compasses you about...even the chains of pride!

Every fear that tries to possess you, every oppression and injustice of man. **Jesus Died for that!!**

Every deep and abiding pain of rejection **Jesus died for it!!!!!**

--Oh Hallelujah!! Because, BEFORE you were formed in your mother's womb - God Knew you and Loved you with an everlasting Love! (God beat the devil to the punch- when we were in our mother's womb, Satan thought he was claiming us -- but God, knew us BEFORE the devil ever had a chance to put his mark on us. **Jesus Died (and Rose, again), so that, you could be ACCEPTED in the Beloved.**

Every act of evil was Laid on Jesus, for He was Bruised for our iniquities and Wounded for our transgressions, and even by His Stripes we are Healed. He Puts our sins away from us as far as the east is from the west, and when He Washes our sins away, we Become white as snow. **This is why I am filled with PRAISE - for His Power and His Grace.**

You Give me back the Strength to Carry on.... for the Angel of the Lord is with me all the days of my life, to Save and Deliver me - and is, even now! Hallelujah!
I am Filled with HIS Praise.

DREAM BIG

Let my dreams come to me,
No mediocrity for me,
For I Serve a BIG GOD,
And HE has BIG Plans for me:

To Give out in different ways
All that He has Put in me,
All these many days -

I will Follow His Plan
For that is the only way to go,
Not the will of man.

So many aspirations
So many desires,
I have not always had
The understanding
Of all He desired;

A NEW DREAM
Was conceived
In me tonight:

Bring that Powerhouse about,
Finance it by Your Power and Might,
A place of Strength,
A place of PRAISE,
For whoever chooses to come that way -
And even a place of rest and relaxation,
Let it be a vacation;

We'll praise Your Name, We'll praise Your Name
While reaching high,
While stretching and lengthening
Those inner and outer thighs.

You said to Dream big,
I'm doing just what YOU said,
YOU Said to a woman once,
Your Faith has made you Whole,
And to another,
So be it unto you, as you Believe.

No longer can they tell me "no,"
When I know it's YOU that Said So -
And those that Offer You Praise
Glorifies YOU,
And I am glad to do so!

While taking care of these temples
In an educated way,
Offering information that could save their day -
All the while,
Giving Praise to YOU
And reaching HIGH.

READY FOR A CHANGE

I've been here too long,
Change my circumstances -
I'm trying to keep my Song,
So far I've been staying pretty Strong,
To God be the Glory!

The devil he has thrown a lot my way,
But it's True,
God Yahweh, is Greater,
And I WILL see a Better day.

For I have learned to Trust Him,
No matter what comes my way -
Yes, it has been a long
And tedious day -
For thirteen years -
One long, tedious way.

But the Angel of Lord
Has Carried me all the way,
And God's Grace has been there
Each and every day!

LOST IN THIS MAZE

Lord, I'm so lost in this maze
I am so confused
I feel so dazed
Which way
Do I turn - What do I do?

I am calling on YOU
Tell me what to do.

I'm so close
I have my hand on the door-knob
But I do not know the combination
To make it all work,
Lord, I am here before You,
As I sob;

I do not know how to pull it all together,
Would You send me a brother
To help me and Guide me
And tell me the things that are Higher;

Time is short,
It's late - but not too late,
Too many hindering spirits,
It's too hard for me,
Too lonely -
Too isolated, but I am trying to Break Free.

Please, Lord
Do not let this Blessed time pass me by

Pull it together for me
Unto YOU I Cry;

For YOU Move heaven and earth
When we cry out to YOU;
This What is within me,
It must give Birth!
It must! It must!!

Do not let this Harvest
Happen without me,
Grant all the Resources Needed,
And the Wisdom -
This is my Plea.
By Your Grace
As I Seek Your Face.

You Tell me to Hold on,
In my humanness
I say, okay, but for how long?

Then time goes by
And Your Spirit Cries
"NOW, now is the time,
Now is the time,"
You Cry!

There are things I need to understand
Dilemmas that need Answers,
They demand.
I realize they come from You
And not totally from the arm of man,
These answers I Command.

Break through this wall
Of fear and setback
I must have Faith, I must make it Work, I will not lack!
Through Your Spirit only -
Go before me, Make this crooked path straight,
Yes, that's it -
You will make this crooked path Straight!
Make it Right, Lord
As only YOU can Do.
Things we don't understand,
When I don't knowYour Plan;
By Your Power
By Your Working
That's far above us,
In mans' misleading
That has caused such a fuss!

You Will Give Grace for the hour
By Your Wisdom and Your Power
You Will Give the Right words to say,
For by this the Fruit of the lips will Save the day;
Again, Break ALL hindering spirits
That would cause harm to Your Plan,
All hindering spirits that would block the way!

Break the curse and the curses
That are holding me back
For I am totally on Your side
Take away the lack;
By the Blood of Jesus,
Take away this lack!

For I am Blessed and not cursed -
I Will have Faith now,
You take it from here
For I know You are Faithful,
This You have made clear!
Your Power Exceeds that of any other,
You are far Above any chain or fetter
That wants to wrap around us
From within and without -
I know this right well,
I have no doubt!

HE MAKES ME LONELY

I'm lonely when he's gone
And long for him to come home;
But he comes home
And I'm lonely still.

Whatever that is in his soul,
The stuff that causes him agony,
And shows he's not Whole.

Since he is apparently
Not willing to deal with it,
It only makes me wish
For him to go,
But I wish him no ill.

No telling the pain
That is there,
From such a long time, ago -
In this absurd asinine way
The behavior that he shows.

I feel so trapped,
But I believe that,
Things are bound to Change,
And to be re-arranged;
It's a bit scary,
Things can get hairy,
And I'm not certain how it will all be.

But God tells me not to worry,
And not to fear,
For He Himself will Take Good Care
Of me,
And my circumstances He Will Steer -
Yes Lord, I will not fear!

For You are quite Capable
Of Taking Care of Your Own,
And as long as I stay with YOU
I am right where I Belong!

For You Govern in the affairs of man,
And even though I have been
To hell and back -
You have Held me safely
In Your Omnipotent Hand.

Many devils I have had to fight,
Even thus far,
It's been an incredibly long road,
And many scars – but I Hold on tight!

It's been difficult
And it's been hard,
But one Awesome thing
I have Seen,
And that is, Jesus has been with me -
And even causes me to Sing,
And even Taught me to shout to His Name,
With the voice of Triumph,
Instead of defeat and shame -
He Has Given me Joy when I wanted to weep,
And Beauty for ashes,

Instead of pain and misery,
And Given me a Song to Sing,
Even in night!
Because He's Making all things Right.

This is why I Know that He is Real,
This is why I want to Show how I feel,
I Want to tell everyone I see,
I want to tell the world
What Jesus Has Done for me!!

THE HEART OF HIS SPIRIT

I am trying Lord
To follow Your Lead,
I even asked you Lord
Be my Guide, be my Lead -

"But My child
You are not following The Heart of My Spirit,
This is how I Lead" -
Lord, I'm so sorry, I will Follow You,
I will Listen to the Heart of YOU,
Just Tell me what to Do -

I know I have missed so many opportunities,
Already, thus far,
"You should be further along,
Than you already, are."

My heart aches,
To Fulfill what my Dreams can tell,
It just doesn't seem like the time is here -
Will it ever be? Yes, it must be, it must Come
After all this time; It Will, it Will:
All that I have Dreamed,
All that I have spelled out,
In written and in verbal form -
And more, much more;

The time is here, the time is now,
For God to do His Mighty Acts
By His Power -

And so much more
Than what I can say or imagine in this hour,
This is what the God of Creation
Is Saying;

It Will now Come to me,
What I have Sown for - what I have Believed for;
And the evil-one
He cannot stop it -
I truly want to be
A powerhouse of generosity.

YOU truly are Faithful in all YOUR Ways,
You are Good to YOUR Children
And to those who Trust in You –
It's True –
You only Want to Do us Good,
If we would only Do what we Should,
If we would only Do what we Should.

Thanks be to YOU GOD
For YOUR Awesomeness,
You are truly Worthy of all our Praise!

IT'S NOT IN VAIN

Thank you Paula
And Christian T.V.
For Speaking to me;
And many others, I have Listened to.

You are my constant mentors
Day after day,
Because I had no one else
To Show me the way -

I know it sounds sad,
But that's just the way it sometimes is -
It's the kind of life I have had to live,
But God!
He is faithful and He is True,
He's not a man that He should lie,
He Teaches us Himself,
Through His Spirit
And He has so Powerfully used you!

He Gets us through
All these hellacious
And turbulent times,
When all we can do
Is sigh and cry.
But I know from all of this hurt and pain,
And when the spirit of the evil-one sends confusion, storms and
rain,
That just keeps on coming,
Again and again;

I know that God's Help
Is all that I Need,
I heard it all of my life,
But I didn't know it was real or true,
Until it was my Plea!

I just have to Praise Him, now -
For HE is so Awesome and Great to me,
Something one might not know about,
Till they open their heart
And See -

And Pray -
And His Spirit and Power
Just take over from there,
And He Leads the way-
All we have to do -
Is Pray!

And follow HIM
Each and every day.

It's not all cut and dry,
Or as easy as it might sound -
(Just the opposite)
Of feeling like you are going to drown;
Rock'n and reel'n
Feel'n like you're not on steady ground,
When you're going through all these trials,
You cover a lot of miles.

But just like Jesus
Did for Peter,
And stretched out His Mighty Hand

While he Walked on the water,
He (Peter) Looked to the Right Man -
He, Jesus, Kept him from drowning
In all the tempestuous weather.

So, it is for us,
If only we would let Him,
Calm our storms
And bring Peace within -

And let Him into our lives,
We would be shocked beyond belief
Of all the Good
He would Bring Forth,
And counteracts the lies -
And Brings down the weapons formed against us,
Because He is For us;

If we could only Learn
To Trust Him,
For Miracles and Power
To be Birthed here on this earth!

DEVINE DESIGN

My troubles and problems,
The ones of which I say,
I can't seem to solve them,
Are made by a Devine Design -
Made by God,
A view not too,
Popular by one or two;

Criticisms and lies
They are formed -
God did not say
It would not be so,
It's okay, because they
Will not prosper,
This I have come to know -
Because no weapon formed against me can prosper,
And every tongue that rises against me,
He will condemn.

This is something we're not sure of,
Or fully understand;
So, somehow, someway
In His eternal Plan
He Sovereignly Works things out
Not according to man:
HE WILL Do it!

We need to trust Him, all the way through it -
Even through the stuff and mess,
And His Angel will pursue them

This you must Confess,
In Jesus Name,
And they are Released
To Bring Forth the same, of what we Profess.

I will lift up my voice in Praise
For it is the Voice of "Grace"
That silences the devil's sound,
And now, you can take your stand in Victory,
GLORY TO GOD!

So, I Declare and Decree it,
Even though I have yet to See it,
The devil has to give back to me
What he has stolen, so relentlessly -
And now it has to be
Double fold,
And Overflowing,
Coming to me.

Not only,
Everything else like Joy, Peace and Happiness,
Which Jesus Gives me in the middle of this mess,
But also, houses, land, and finances too,
And much more than I can say -
I look forward to that day!
And can hardly Wait to see what the Lord will Do!
For He is Doing it now,
It is Coming my way!

I SURRENDER

I have to remember,
Because to YOU I surrender -
The Best Is Yet To Come.

So, whatever the future paths hold,
I trust YOU,
As YOU are the One Who Teaches us,
And continues to make us Whole;

And to him (or her) to whom much is Given
Much shall be Required,
And Lord YOU definitely have Given me much -

I want to remember it all,
I want to responsibly give away
What YOU have so Faithfully
And Awesomely, Deposited into me -
For You have Given me Your Call.

I have not turned away,
But instead,
Have run head long
Seeking after You
And Your Wisdom,
Even though it seems so long -
I have not been head strong -
But rather tried to take on the meek
And humble role
That You say we should let unfold,
And strive to develop these traits;

It will keep us straight!

It has all been so breathtaking and Wondrous-
Your Glory I have sSeen
And experienced
Even to a small degree, I'm sure -
Though it seemed quite awesome and spectacular
At the time -
Even though I might not understand
All that YOU were doing
And all that You were up to,
And all that You had Planned;
And even all that YOU allowed -
This might be the most difficult of all -
For at times, many things seemed to go sour;
It is a good thing that I vowed -
For You have Taught me of the Power;

For it was YOU that Taught me
That the devil is a liar;
I know that he is -
YOUR Anointed ones know it also,
They're the ones YOU have used to Teach it,
Through Your Holy Spirit.

For these dilemmas in life,
I pray for an Answer:
For with YOU is Wisdom
With YOU is great Strength;

Lord, if we do not Help each other,
Then what Hope is there?
For the devil hates us all
And not only wants us to fall,

But locks into a scheme and plan
To make that happen ----

But I thank YOU that it is True,
That now, no weapon formed against me will prosper,
This is from You,
And ANY tongue that rises against me in judgment,
YOU will Condemn -

That deserves a hallelujah,
And as long I travel with YOU
I am never bored -
For I can hardly keep up,
As it is -
My Prayer is, don't let me miss
All that YOU Have for me;

And Do Bring down the enemy, O Lord,
And his treacherous, scheming ways.
I am so ready to be blessed,
I Want Your Best!

I do not know why
You have waited till this time in my life,
To Show me Your Glory,
And Turn my life around,
But at least, Your Life I have found,
I will go from here, and will not fear -
But I will Build upon what You have Put
on the inside of me,
Knowing I have been Called
for such a time as this.

PRAISE'N YOU

Lord, Tell me what to do -
I'm Praise'n YOU;

I'm try'n to do my work,
But I have so much to do,
I don't know what to do, first.

I have got to Focus, You said,
To Walk this path in this dark cave,
Trust'n that You Guide every step -
But what if I mess up?

Just one step at a time,
You Said;
Am I really walking on a dime?
Do not look to the left or to the right,
Just look straight ahead -
Then when you get to the end of your flight
You will see why it took MY Might...

Yes, Lord, but I See it now,
Times where I feel I am walking on that bow,
Times where I feel the devils
Trying to creep in
Seeing their slimy hands
Reaching for me, trying to make me bend – not because they're
in me, because they are not;
It's Jesus that's my Lot – HE is the Alpha & Omega, the Beginning
& the End,
And HE's the One on Whom I Depend.

I know that the thief,only comes to kill, steal and destroy -
You Said he is now coming in for the kill,
Lord, this could make anyone feel ill -
This is no ploy;

But I will Continue
To Confess one thing,
And that is, Lord,
YOU are my King,
YOU are Lord Over everything -

Even though we still live in this wicked world,
You make the Difference in this girl;
You have Shown and Given to me Your Love,
Something I did not quite know before,
And TRULY Your Peace,
Just like a Dove -
That's really something,
When you have had neither for too long,
Nor have you been able to claim a Song -

So many people have said to me,
You look so sad,
I wonder what your misery could be,
Why can't you be glad -

But just as we hear in some of the rich songs,
Jesus really is the Answer for my Song -
It took me so long,
But I know there are Reasons for everything,
And He Governs in the affairs of man,
And I am Tapping into that Plan.

I can finally say,
I have a Song,
And Jesus is the Reason for that Song.

I can't figure out why it took me so long,
To Connect with this Love,
That has Changed my life,
And Given me a Song -

A New Song, A Song of Deliverance and Freedom
A Song of Happiness and Joy,
Things I have never had before -
Even though there is no earthly reason,
To be feeling this way,
But YOU and YOUR Spirit have Said,
That if I were to just keep on PRAISE'N YOU
Everything Would be Alright
Everything Would Come along.

And I Believe this Lord,
For You are not a man that You should lie -
I am Showing my Faith by my works,
I am PRAISE'N YOU
Even when it hurts -
Even when there's still pain in my life,
And everything seems to be going through the night;
But Thanks be to God,
You are the Rock that is Sure,
Your Blood keeps us Pure,
And Your Promises will Come through:
I will Keep on PRAISE'N YOU -
You are Faithful and You are True:
I will keep on Praise'n YOU!!

WALK'N ON WATER - IT'S GONNA BE ALRIGHT

I'm walk'n on water
Yeah, Yeah
I'm walk'n on water,
Yeah, Yeah
It's gonna be alright,
It's gonna be alright;

I've got my eyes on Jesus,
I've got my eyes on Jesus,
Yeah, Yeah
It's gonna be alright,
He's take'n me through this night
Yeah, Yeah,
I'm walk'n on water
I'm walk'n on water
It's gonna be alright -

I'm not look'n to the left or right,
He's Take'n me through this night
He's gonna make everything all right,
He's gonna make everything alright,
Everything's gonna be alright,
Everything's gonna be alright;

The enemy's gonna take flight,
And I'm gonna Win this fight
Yeah, Yeah,
I'm walk'n on water

Everything's gonna be alright,
I've got my eyes on Jesus,
He's gonna Make it all right;

He's make'n it all right,
I'm walk'n on water
Yeah, Yeah,
I'm walk'n on water
Yeah, Yeah –

Everything's gonna be alright,
Yeah, Yeah
Everything's gonna be all Right,
Everything's gonna be Alright!!

I'VE BEEN GIVEN REVELATION

I'm not looking at my situation
For God has given me revelation
That everything's going to be alright,
No matter what it may look like, tonight.

I might have to keep crying
For just a little while longer,
But I know that He is with me,
And my faith is now so much stronger;

He has Told me to stop my crying
That He has Heard my cries
And Seen my tears,
And that He is Getting Ready
To Restore the years,
That the locust and canker worm
Have eaten,
And that I need to Get Ready
For double;

Double prosperity,
No matter if you like that word or not,
I will soon look back and say,
Look what the Lord has Wrought;

My spirit no longer needs to feel beaten,
For I will soon Walk in the Victory
That He has Promised, And Do even now -
Because I Trust in YOU oh Lord,
And YOU are True,
I Will be Rewarded, too.

HE CARES FOR ME - HE CARES FOR YOU

I do not know
What is about to happen,
But I hear God's Voice
In such a strong way,
Telling me
Do not give in, do not give in -
Fight, fight, fight – Fight the Good Fight of Faith
And you will Win;

No matter what is going to happen,
No matter what I will feel,
He's Saying to me,
I Care about you,
I AM ah, so Real!

I Care for you,
I AM Concerned,
Truly and deeply
Concerned for you -
Thank you Lord, I Know You Do.

I know He Cares for me,
And since HE Cares so
For me,
I know He deeply
Cares for others too -

And what HE has Done for me,
He Can and Will Do for them,
If only they will Trust
And Believe HIM!

But they Must first, Hear,
In order to Believe,
So I say,
Here I am Lord,
Send me!

HE'S TAKING ME THROUGH - TO BLESS YOU

He's been taking me through hellious times
To be a Blessing to you;
I've been fighting many devils (on the outside not the inside
of me),
But I know God is True –
This I have lived and Seen, too.

The many things I have been going through
Allows me to say,
If He Does it for me,
He Can and Will Do it for you -

I will not lie but admit,
That it has been so very hard
And I have wanted to quit;
But in my hurt, confusion and pain,
The Lord just has His Way
Of Coming to us in all of it,
And Says to us
"Do not quit,"
I AM your God,
You are My child
Just keep Holding on a little while;

"For I AM with you,
Do not fear or be dismayed,
I will Hold you with MY Righteous Right Hand
Even though things look delayed."

"I AM your God
You are Mine,
I have Made Covenant with you,
Do Everything I Say;
I Will Lead you and Guide you continually
I Will Show you the Way -

I Create the storm
The winds and the waves
You are now walking through,
And the fire, but it will not harm you,
Nor the floods overflow you;

I Want you to Know
That the trouble
You are now walking in,

That I Will Be the One to Deliver you,
And not, any person or friend."

So, when I arrive at my Red Sea,
God Has already Said to me,
Stand still and See
The Salvation of the Lord,
I Will Part the waters for you,
Just Wait and See;

So, standing on this side,
I Choose to Believe Him
As I let Him Abide,
Lead and Guide.

As He Has always been Faithful and True,
I remind myself,
"Why should He now fail *you*?
Just keep on Trusting Him
As you walk in Obedience
To Everything He Tells you to Do,
He's not a man that He should lie,
It will all Come to Pass by and by."

CASTING ALL MY CARE

I need intercessors, Lord,
Please Hear my prayer,
How much longer must I go on,
With all these many burdens
Alone to bear?

How long O Lord?
You are Mighty,
I know, to Save
Me from all my troubles,
And I know it is so.

But not for me alone,
That I travail heavy in prayer -
It is for my children
I long for them
In this Awesome Treasure
Of knowing You - to Share!!

Everyone declares,
A host of prayer warriors
They have for themselves -

You are my Jehovah Rapha,
My Awesome Healer,
Of body, mind and soul,
Be the Healer
To my daughter,
You Will Save her,
And Make her Whole;

Jehovah Shama,
The Lord Who Said,
I AM with you
Wherever you go,
Shama, I AM here,
This I want you to know!

My precious daughter and son,
And son in law,
Have yet to know
This Awesome
Comfort, Peace and Joy -
Cause them to Know!
Be to them
What You are to me
And more -

Guide their every footstep,
And Bind what the evil-one might want to do,
And Give them Life, and Abundantly too -
For they have had too many, prayers go up
On their behalf,
Go up to You;
And not a one of them is wasted
For You Hear them all,
And Stir from Your holy hill,
When we call -

I can't wait for the day,
When they say,
"I have Tasted
And Seen that the Lord is Good!"
And already, they are Doing what they Should!

I feel so alone
Sometimes, I feel like I'd rather die,
My heart hurts so bad,
How hard can one cry?

"Hold on, Hold on,"
I keep Hearing Your Spirit Say,
My God I cannot afford
To put myself in delay,
By being discouraged
Today, or any day.

I now **Know**
I am just in a **Process**,
That You are Taking me through -
I have not always felt this agony,
Not always have I had friends
So few;

But You are Sanctifying me,
Through and through,
This I now know;
The road's been rough
And long,
Lonely and hurtful,
And sometimes,
I have misplaced my Song -

But You are Teaching me,
That the arm of flesh
Will surely fail,
Whether it's mine or theirs
We are truly frail -

But upon Your Strong Arm
I am Learning to Lean,
And am surely Finding
That only to You
I need to Cling!

So Thank You, Lord
For these times and trials, sore -
They only make me to Trust You more,
And like an eagle, **Soar!**

I WILL NOT FEAR

My heart is troubled within me, tonight,
What the Prophet said was true,
I knew it was for me, too.

He was talking to me
Just like Samuel,
Being Called to get on his knees-
Before the Light went out.

You are Wanting to Talk to me,
What an Honor and a privilege for me,
To Hear from You,
And I want to Listen & Hear,
I really do -
But what do You want me to say and do?

This is not the first time
You have Said to me:
"Listen! The voice -
The cry of the daughter of My people
From a far country,"

And this is what it is saying:
"Is not the Lord in Zion?
Is not her King in her?"

"The harvest is past,
The summer is ended,
And we are not saved!"

This scares me,
And I Cry out to You
Lord, Lord,
You are my Lord,
What do You Want me to do?
I ask this of You.

For everything
You Say to me
I try and do -
No matter how frightened or scared
I might be,
No matter those hateful and deceitful
Religious spirits,
Come chasing after me,
And hurl their complaints and accusations at me.

I know,
And I thank You,
For Having it all under Control,
Even when I do not understand it all,
And when it is all yet untold,
When it has yet, to all unfold -

It's okay,
Because You Have Told me,
You have my back,
It's okay,
Because I know when
I Trust You I will not lack!

But what about those around me?
And those I dearly love?
You must Save them,

You Must Send Deliverance
From Above!!

I will not doubt Your Word,
Written or Rameh form,
For You have Said,
You will Save them,
And Teach them,
Even though things look forlorn;

And I will not,
I will not fear or dread,
For I have Heard Your
Guiding, Teaching Voice,
That has Said,

"Your fear is the only way
That Satan can work" -
So I will not give him my heart,
He just wants to steal, kill and hurt,
And I now am Learning,
That no weapon
Formed against me can work,
And somehow You Put out
Every lie he is forming,
And even the gossip from ignorant minds that, are burning;
And every false tongue
Rising-up against us,
You will Condemn -

For You have Said this to me,
And Sealed it to my heart,
Time and time again.

So Bind my own fears,
Deliver me from them,
As I Cry out to You,
Let my Faith Build from within,
As You Remind me of Your Word -
And my spirit Renew!

Do not let me speak
Or tell of the things Satan whispers in my ear,
Like David said in the book of Psalms,
You Guard my tongue,
You Take away my fear!

For, again Your prophetic Promise
I Claim,
And to it I Cling,
For it is so Beautiful
I just want to Sing!

As You have Said to My heart
O Lord:
"I have a Covenant with you,
And My Spirit that is upon you,
And the Words I have Put in your mouth
Shall not depart from your mouth,
Nor from your children's mouth,
Nor from your grandchildren's mouth,
From this time on
And forever more!"

For this I Praise You,
I Glorify and Magnify You!
I will not speak fear,
For Your Spirit has Told me to Hear,

What You have to Say on the matter,
And I Will Listen,
And I will have Your Power;

Your Glory will Rise upon me,
Even now in this hour,
For such a time as this,
To Reveal Your Power -
Your Glory Rises over me
To be Seen on me,
And to You,
I Give all the Praise and Glory,
For You alone
Are Worthy!

You Make weak men Strong,
And strong men weak,
You Give our futures Hope,
When they look so bleak.

Your Word that Goes out of Your Mouth,
Shall not return empty and void,
But it shall Accomplish what You Send it to do,
It shall Prosper and Succeed,
For there is no God like You!!

You Form the light and Create darkness,
You Make Peace and Create calamity,
As well,
This is what You Yourself has Said,
But sometimes, others, they cannot tell.

Joseph's brothers,
They, at him hissed,

But God was in Control,
And they missed -
He himself said,
"You meant it to me for evil,
But God Meant it to me for Good,
To Save many people alive."

You fully deserve our Adoration,
Since You Made all of creation -
You Formed us in our mother's womb,
You Know our down sitting
And our uprising,
And even our thoughts afar off,
You are the Alpha and Omega,
The beginning and the end (of things) –
You have it all under control!

LED BY YOUR SPIRIT

I am who, He Says I am,
I am ACCEPTED in the Beloved,
No longer rejected,
No longer smothered -

I am the Righteousness of God,
I am the Apple of His Eye,
He told this to me,
He is not a man that He should lie;

He Gives me Joy,
Even when things are still, yet, wrong,
But He causes me to Sing and Dance,
And I have a brand NEW **song**!!!

He Puts Laughter in my mouth,
Just like it says in Psalms,
It sometimes seems,
Like one who dreams,
I can actually laugh over things -
This is the Work of God!
Hallelujah!!

He's Getting Ready to prosper me,
Like nothing else I've ever seen,
He's Told this to me,
And I **Willingly Believe,**
So it will Come to me:

Pressed down,
Shaken together,
Overflowing -
Abundantly, above all that I ask or think,
According to His Power that Works in me;

And His Power "is" Working in me,
Steadily, Increasing daily,
No matter what those religious devils say;

I will Continue to make room,
For You Holy Spirit,
For it is by You,
The Standard is Raised,
When the enemy of our souls,
Comes in like a flood,
The **Standard of Righteousness,**
Goodness and Justice,
Mercy and Love!!

It is by You,
We can Accomplish many things,
And Exploits -
Not by our strength,
Might and power,
But by Your Spirit.

You Give Direction,
In an important hour,
I want to be Led by You,
And continue to feel Your Power,

Not to quench You ever again,
Let alone Grieve You,
Who Abides within -
For as many who are Led by the Spirit of God,
Are the sons of God! Amen!

I'M TRUST'N IN YOU

Lord, I don't have time
To be discouraged,
I'm Trust'n in You,
Now You do the rest.

Lord, I just want to thank You,
For all You have done for me,
You Yourself have said to me,
"The Angel of My Presence
Has Saved and Delivered you,
And Carried you all the days
Of your life."

Thank You, Lord,
You are so Awesome;

And thank You for what
You are Going to Do,
In Your Perfect Timing -
When all of this is through,
Yes, I understand -

You have Brought me through
So much,
It's hard for one to Believe,
And are bringing me through,
Still,
I just want to Live,
And to Accomplish
All that You Have for me -

Through the Eyes of Faith,
Many things
I can See;

And I know there are good
Surprises on the way,
Because Your Power Works in me,
Even this day,
And You Said,
You Would Do Abundantly,
Exceedingly,
Above all that I could
Ask or even think -

And I have a very creative imagination,
And I have Learned
To draw on Your Restoration,
And Your Word that tells me to Creatively, think,
And it tells me to Ask,
And all that I can Believe You for,
You Would Do,
Because You are Good.

You are Bringing me through,
You have Made me **NEW**;

I've tried to be okay
At every turn,
And for anointed friendships
I really yearn;

And now, I need Your help,
I cry out to You,
I know that You are True,

And there is no God like unto YOU!

In my times of confusion,
In brief moments of darkness of delusion,
In disappointment,
And impatience -
If I Stay Connected to You,
I know it's all going to be Alright,
Because I'm going through a Process,
I'm coming out of this night;

But I still have the Light,
No matter how, I at times, might feel,
Smart people always know that,
Your feelings are not always real;
For they can cause us to rock & reel,
They are not to be trusted,
Just because we "feel" – But to Continue to Trust You!

But You are the One
We are to Trust,
No matter how bleak things might look,
No matter how much disgust;
You are Working a New Thing,
And Bringing
About Your Plan,
And on Your prophetic Promises
I will Stand!

I know You Hear me,
When unto You I Cry,
And this is "why"
I Shout and Sing,
You Cause me to Praise

And Glory in my King!

Nothing else like it
On planet earth,
When God gives you New birth,
And Works in you
A New Thing –
You will Want to Shout and Sing!

You Hear me from Your holy Temple,
This is why I Praise You,
My prayers come even into Your Ears,
You Deliver and Rescue me,
This is why I Trust You,
This is why I Believe -

Every time I have Asked You anything,
You Have always Answered me -
Through sermon, plight or song,
The Written or SpokenWord,
Now to You I Belong! Amen.

I CAN GET THROUGH ANY STORM

I Can get through any storm with Jesus, for the Lord will guide me continually, and satisfy my soul in drought, and strengthen my bones;

I shall be like a watered garden, and like a spring of water whose Waters do not fail. My leaf also shall not wither, and whatsoever I do, I shall Prosper - because I Trust and Follow Him (Jesus) The Messiah, the True Savior of the world, and follow His Commands & Obey Him...He Protects and Guides me from harm, and Leads me to my desired haven, because I Call out to Him --

He Died on the Cross of Calvary for my sins, Heals my broken heart, and Binds up all my wounds, Gives me New Life, a Song, a Future and a Hope, and quickly Subdues all my enemies --

I Wrap myself in His Word and His Truth, and I do not depart from the Words He has Put in my mouth, nor do my children depart from His Words, nor will my grandchildren depart from the Words He Puts in their mouths - and they are Blessed of Him and will Inherit the earth, and **every** curse is Broken off of them, so that they may Prosper, and He Calls them by name, and I also, to Give us a Future and a Hope;

I will Live and not die, to Proclaim what the LORD Has Done - for He is Married to me, has Made an Oath with me, and will Fulfill His Covenant with me...He has Passed by me and Saw me struggling in my own blood and Said to me LIVE, yes, He Saw me struggling in my own blood, and said to me LIVE"

He is Making me to Thrive like a plant in the field, I am Growing & Maturing and Becoming very Beautiful... but still feel just a little naked & bare, but He is Passing by me again, and Sees this is my Season of LOVE and is Spreading His Wing over me to COVER me (Hallelujah!) for He has Sworn an Oath to me and Entered into a Covenant with me, and I Became His; He Carries me and Delivers me all the days of my life - He Puts a Wall of Fire around me, so that evil cannot touch me!

He Tells me to not touch the unclean thing, and that the Glory of the Lord will be Seen in my midst, and Will Be my Rear-Guard...He Loves me with an Everlasting Love, Satisfies me with Goodness; and His Mercies are New every morning!!!

He Puts a Song in my mouth, a New, Song - a Song of Deliverance and Praise -- even Praise unto my God and Laughter in my mouth.

YOUR CHILDREN TAUGHT BY THE LORD

ISAIAH 54:13-17

"All your children shall be Taught by the Lord, and Great shall be the Peace of your children.

In Righteousness you shall be Established; you shall be far from oppression, for you shall not fear; (and you shall be far from) terror, for it shall not come near you. Indeed, they shall surely assemble, but not because of Me. Whoever, assembles against you shall fall for your sake.

Behold, I have Created the blacksmith who blows the coals in the fire, who brings forth an instrument for his work; and I have Created the spoiler to destroy.

No weapon formed against you shall prosper; and every tongue that rises against you in judgment you shall Condemn. This is the Heritage of the servants of the Lord and their Righteousness is from ME, Says the Lord!!!"

IN CLOSING -

Be Focused on the Promises of God that Come'n
Don't be focused on what's around you;
Get a New Attitude -
You were Born for a God-Given Purpose and Destiny.
You have POWER on the inside of you (as a Child of the Most
High GOD)!!
You have Everything you need to Live a Life of Victory -
You just need to GET-UP out of your misery!
Why sit there til you die?
Quit asking 'why,' 'why?!'
And start Pressing-in, for the Prize
And you Will Win -
So, dry your eyes
And See yourself
Living your Dream
And Look for the Hope of the Prize of the High-Calling in Christ
And you Will Have
What you Believe!!!

Amen!

DESTINED AND APPOINTED FOR BEAUTY

Isaiah 61:3

"To Appoint unto them that mourn in Zion, to give unto them Beauty for ashes, the Oil of Joy for mourning, the Garment of Praise for the spirit of heaviness."

O God of heaven - I have been Appointed for **BEAUTY,** I have been Destined for Joy (who would have guessed it? who would have known?) Before I was even formed in my mother's womb, even though, my mourning seemed to last a lifetime: Joy Comes in the morning time, after the long dark night - when we Trust in God our Savior - The night will not always last -- when He becomes our Joy, and we Rejoice in Him, He Rewards us with Himself, and that Releases Joy unspeakable and so Full of Glory, it is then that, I Fulfill my Appointment to the Garment of PRAISE, instead of depression and heaviness, pain and misery.

With the Fruit of my lips I will offer the Sacrifice of Thanksgiving and the Sacrifice of Praise! For He is Worthy to be Praised; He is Worthy of all my Praise; His faithfulness Endures to every generation and His Mercies are New every morning!! I sleep in Peace and awake each day - I look around to see that He Loads me down with Benefits in every way! *He Forgives all my transgressions, Heals all my diseases and Redeems my life from destruction, and Crowns me with His Loving Kindness & Tender Mercies.*

For having such Forgiveness and Mercy toward me, and Putting His Love on me - for Speaking **"Life"** to me when death was breathing down my neck, for *Restoring my life,* for Guiding me through the valley of the shadow of death, and Taking my fears away, *because* I **Trusted in Him** and **He Comforted and Protected** me everyday; and because the Angel of the Lord Guided me and Protected me and Carried me ALL the days of my life!!! (Halllelujah)!!

I Will **Praise** Him because, **HE Has ACCEPTED** _me_ in the BELOVED and has Loved me with an Everlasting Love; I Will **PRAISE Him** because He has Married me and Made an Everlasting Covenant with me; because He has Planned to Give me a Future and a Hope, (and all His Plans and Purpose Will Be Fulfilled); because His Thoughts toward me are for Good and not for evil; because I Trust in Him and must be Careful to Observe to Do all that He Commands me to Do...no matter what anyone else might think or say...I will say, "thus, Says the Lord;" I only want to Please Him, as He Takes Good Care of His Own and Rewards those who diligently Seek Him, and Brings Blessing on those who Obey Him, and cursing upon those who do not - No matter the lies of Satan and man: **Let God be True** and every man a liar.

Put on your Beautiful Garments: those Beautiful Garments of 'PRAISE'
Those Beautiful Garments of Righteousness
Those Beautiful Garments of Holiness (be holy for I AM Holy, says the LORD);
Those Beautiful Garments of **PEACE** (HE Will Keep you in **Perfect PEACE**, whose mind is stayed (Kept) on HIM (the LORD).

(PEACE I Give to you, not as the world gives, I Give to you, Jesus Said).

Those Beautiful Garments of LOVE (For I have Commanded you, to LOVE one another, Says the LORD) and Perfect LOVE, (the God-kind-of-LOVE, through the POWER and Grace of the Holy Spirit) Casts out fear.

Put on the Beautiful Garments of JOY (do not sorrow, for **the Joy of the LORD** is your **STRENGTH).**

(Rejoice in the LORD, always - again, I say REJOICE = Re-Joy: having Joy over & over, again) GOD ('the LORD) **Gives you and me Permission to be Joyful !!!**

In other words, we don't have to feel guilty about being "Joyful."
*** **It's okay to let yourself feel "Joy"** ***
Take Joy (the Spirit of Joy) Allow it – Embrace it! (Know that's "okay" even if you're not used to it).

"Be anxious for nothing, but in everything by prayer and supplication, with thanksgiving let your requests be known to GOD; And the **PEACE** of God ... will Guard your hearts and minds through Jesus Christ."
Philippians 4: 6, 7

*Having the "Peace of GOD" gives us "Joy."
We don't have to hold onto "worry," "anger," "fear," "guilt," "regrets," or any of that!
Rejoice in your GOD - the One and Only God of the Universe Yahweh, the Maker of Heaven and earth!
"Therefore, my beloved and longed for ... my Joy & Crown, so, **Stand Fast in the LORD..."** Amen.
(Philippians 4:1)

Praising the Lord (even when they are not the way that, they should be) **Changes you on the inside!**
The more we Praise and (it turns to Worship) of the One & Only True and Living God, the more that, we **"Change!"**

115

It Changes us little by little, bit by bit, piece by piece – instead of a slow fade – it's more of a slow Enlightenment, a slow intensity, a slow Brilliance Beginning to happen!!

When you (and I) CHANGE on the inside – then ALL Things are Possible (in and through Christ)!!! (The Lord Jesus Christ is the Only One Who Can Change us)!!!

Now, unto Him Who is Able to Do Exceedingly, Abundantly, Above all that, we ask or think, According to the POWER that, Works in us! Ephesians 3:20

Let the Redeemed of the Lord, Say so!
I Praise Him in the Sanctuary;
Let all those who Trust in the Lord, Praise Him!
PRAISE HIM in the morning, PRAISE HIM in the afternoon and PRAISE HIM in the evening!!
The LORD RULES, HE REIGNS – HE is Worthy to Be PRAISED!

LET ALL THE NATIONS PRAISE THE LORD!!! AMEN.

Printed in the United States
by Baker & Taylor Publisher Services